My Angel Gabriel
My Autistic Angel

Aida Santiago

authorHOUSE®

AuthorHouse™
1663 Liberty Drive, Suite 200
Bloomington, IN 47403
www.authorhouse.com
Phone: 1-800-839-8640

First published by AuthorHouse 2/23/2009

ISBN: 978-1-4389-4046-5 (sc)

Library of Congress Control Number: 2009901779

Printed in the United States of America
Bloomington, Indiana

This book is printed on acid-free paper.

Translation by Frieda Varon

AKNOWLEDGMENTS

Gabriel, my family, and myself thank Frieda Varon for her gift of love translating the book into the English version. Also, Margarita Plascencia for editing, and finally Peter Bayer for proof reading the final draft. You all are contributors in our effort to defeat this syndrome. God Bless You.

INTRODUCTION

My Angel Gabriel is dedicated to all autistic children who, without knowing, are patiently waiting for someone with a gigantic determination, who will do them justice, and will return to them that which was unscrupulously taken from them.

In order to achieve this, one has to report the cause of of this disturbance provoked in such insensitive and devastating way. Possibly, through ignorance, we ourselves contribute to this evil, which terrorizes parents and destroys others.

As part of society it is our responsibility to help those who, day by day, confront this situation. We are able to do so much! To ignore it is not an option. We do not know who will be next. One step, one consideration, can make the difference. The enemy has no name, we do not know where it comes from, nor where it is going. We do know that we can defend ourselves knowing the means by which we can help to minimize the permanent damage that these angels are exposed to; who like Gabriel, do not give up and struggle to overcome their limitations whatever they may be.

Here is the manner in which we confronted this evil. It is not a guide, but it sheds a light that may illuminate the road for others to take even though their conditions may be different.

There is a light at the end of the tunnel... a hope for autistic children.

DEDICATION

Gabriel's attention, happiness and hope is always directed to his mother. Her mere presence gives him strength and security, by her side there is neither sadness nor confusion for him, his world shines with the love he receives from her. This is evidenced by the display of caresses and kisses that Gabriel showers her with every time he has the opportunity. He lacks the language to express this, but it is not necessary; there are no words that envelop the reach and grandeur of these sublime sentiments, those that emanate from God. That is why I dedicate this book to her: From Gabriel, with his little heart full of gratitude, to Cindy, his mother.

Contents

CHAPTER 1

THE DIAGNOSIS

We left there with a knot in our stomach. We did not exchange words. We were overwhelmed by an indescribable pain. There was not an expression spoken, neither short nor long, in this world, that embraced what we felt. The grieving in our soul did not let up. I understood what the poet says...

> "There are strikes in life so strong... I do not know,
> strikes like the wrath of God, like if before them,
> the accumulation of the life's suffering flooded the soul...I do not know"
>
> [my translation]
> (César Vallejo)

God is not a God of hate. It is impossible that this pain comes from anything besides love. The pain we felt was born from love.

As we walked with our heads bent through that hallway our looks crossed.

A mother was waiting next to a wheelchair with a son or daughter, I do not remember. The picture was impressing. An icy dagger went through my heart. The child, about six years old, had his little head supported by a brace and his little body was held in a reclining position by some straps across his chest. I do not know what my daughter thought. I do not know if she feared for Gabriel's future. I only remember that my heart broke in a thousand pieces and I thanked the Lord. Thank You, God, that Gabriel is able to walk, that his muscles and body are strong. Thanks because it could have been worse. Thank You for being here. I sang or rather silently recited a chorus I had learned many years ago:

"How good it is to praise
God when all goes well,
How good it is to praise God
when there are no problems in life,
what a good thing!

But I praise him in the breakdown
because Holy Christ is glorified
 within me."

I took my baby's little hand and hugged him. He had no idea of the world which was collapsing around him. Lord, do not abandon him!

The way back was filled with a sensation of emptiness and helplessness. We arrived home and became involved in the task of feeding Gabriel. My daughter had to go to work. She said goodbye and left. I was now left with worries about my daughter. My daughter, Gabriel's mother, had to feel even worse than I did, her pain was bigger. How to face this new dilemma! How many thoughts must have crossed her mind! She did not return till early evening.

In the afternoon my husband, the grandfather, arrived.

- What? How did it go with Gabriel?

I started to cry, I could not utter a word.

- The doctors say that he is autistic.

- What? Are they sure?

- Yes... there was a group comprised of a psychologist, a social worker, a speech therapist, and a physical therapist.

- How do they know?

- They observed him; they gave him some activities to do, etc. They say that they noticed it when he was entering by his absent look, fixed, without noticing anyone a 'funneled' look, they say.

We embraced each other.

It was October 7th, 2004. Gabriel was 2 years and 4 months old.

In the evening my oldest daughter Aisha, come with a cake for her father's birthday. She entered the room. I gave her the news in tears. She consoled me telling me that in the school where she works there are autistic children who are "fine", that they learn.

My younger son also called to congratulate his father. He cried...cried inconsolably, like he had never done with his son. I do not know what my son said to him.

I spoke to my oldest son, Riqui, and he told me something I will never forget:

-To what point is it something bad? Autistic children are honest children, they do not know how to lie, and they act with kindness. Some are intelligent, so let's hope.

I told all the siblings to talk to their sister. It was something new, unknown.

Nothing consoles a mother whose deepest hopes and dreams rest in a future filled with happiness, triumphs, and big conquests for her son. It is a longing to delight in with the expectation that some day, he will have a happy and fulfilled life. To consider the possibilities, remain ignorant, fear the uncertainty in a future which one does not know how to face, is devastating, especially when it deals with a child. It is like removing the earth from under one's feet. Now what? What do we do?

Notes

CHAPTER 2

RETROSPECTION

Last May, Gabriel started to change. He used to be an active child, happy and always investigating everything. His first year was 'normal' and he crawled on time. As all children of his age, he took out all the pots of the cabinets and played in an organized fashion. He fell off his tricycle. He started to talk. In the afternoons, his grandfather used to take him for a walk before dinner. He used to throw balls on the tennis court, swing on the swing or play in the swimming pool.

In April he got sick with a very bad virus. He was ill for a few days. He took antibiotic until he finished the bottle. He had not yet completely recuperated, when we took a trip that had been planned, for a family reunion with our son in Illinois. He spent a few miserable days with temper tantrums and constantly crying. We thought it was part of the virus. The worst was yet to come.

In May, he began to have lapses in which he appeared not to hear us. The babysitter, who took care of him, could not manage to keep him seated to eat. He started to watch television through the reflection in the mirror. He would climb on anything and did not seem to fear any danger.

- What happened to Gabriel's thigh?

- I do not know, he was in the room and came out with that wound.

- But, didn't he cry?

- No, I saw it bleeding.

- It's a large, deep wound. It is impossible that it does not hurt him.

He simply didn't feel the pain. Until today, three years later, the scar remains as a reminder.

By June he started to cry without any apparent reason. He did not want to stand up. He would lie down on the floor instead.

Putting him to bed was a dilemma. He did not know how to position himself to go to sleep. He found it difficult to fall asleep. We thought that

14

he was waiting for his mother to come home from work to lie down next to him.

At the same time the babysitter resigned because she was going to have a bably so we attributed a lot to the fact that he missed her. What a mistake!

In the month of June we moved to Royal Palm Beach, since I had retired from my job as a teacher. After that, I left on a trip to San Antonio to correct Advanced Placement Spanish Exams as part of a job with the College Board, for one week. When I returned Gabriel was absent. He did not seem to be aware of where he was nor who we were. He did not hear us. He was obsessed with television; it appeared to be the only thing that held his interest. His only toys were those that had lights or went around in circles. We tried to comprehend his behavior. We hoped it was all part of a stage. Not all children are the same.

- My little grandchild is a perfectionist. He tries to see things from different perspectives. He is very inquisitive. He turns his head back or sideways to look at objects. Sometimes he walks and tries to see things passing by as if he were studying centrifugal laws.

Was it denial? No, it was plain and simple ignorance.

In September, there was a hurricane in Florida. It was necessary to leave the house. We were running late packing. The hurricane would arrive the following day at 10:00 AM.

We went north to the house of a relative. The trip was to take 3 hours. It took 14 hours! The highways and roads Northbound and Westbound were blocked. We had to turn off the air conditioning to save on gas. There was a sea of carbon dioxide. The lines at the gas stations were unending. My God, when will we arrive? Gabriel fell asleep at about 12:00AM. We arrived at 5:00AM.!

Our baby was completely disoriented. While there, he licked everything. In a split second he could be lying on the floor, licking it. On the second day we gave him rice and beans with pork. In the evening he started to vomit. He was writhing with pain. Every time he bent over to vomit he had a bowel movement, horrible diarrhea. The following day he did not want to eat anything. He did not know whom to approach to pick him up.

We decided to return home. The trip back was not so bad. Gabriel rested enough.

Upon arrival, he went into his room, sat down on his chair and started to rock his body back and forth. I asked myself why he would be doing this. I thought he still had a stomach ache.

Nothing important had happened to the house. We exposed the child to this trauma for no reason. They were three horrible days locked up. Who would have known?

We decided to take Gabriel to his new pediatrician. She was a young female doctor, with insight. She recommended that we take Gabriel to a speech therapist, since my daughter expressed her concern that he did not yet speak.

I had already begun to worry since I noticed something abnormal in his behavior. I had commented to my daughter in law, who is like a daughter, that I thought that Gabriel had something like Attention Deficit Disorder. We were very worried about how my daughter would take this.

Today, I wish that it had been only that!

Now we were there. The psychologist asked my daughter:

- Why are you bringing the child here?

- I am worried because he does not speak.

- It is not only that. Your child is autistic.

He said this bluntly and without showing sensitivity. He dropped the weight of the world on my daughter's shoulders. It was the weight of a mother's pain for her child. One should respect a mother's pain. It is the ache from the biggest and noblest love that could exist. No one knows what love is until one has a child. May those who do not have one forgive me, but there is no comparison, for as much as you love your spouse, your parents or your nephews, you cannot know.

My daughter bent over and moaned quietly. She asked to go to the bathroom.

When she returned, the psychologist continued to say;

> - From what we have observed, we have placed your son at this level on the scale. That is to say, that his autism is quite severe.

He showed us the top of the scale.

And here we are with our Gabriel. We stood up. We were not defeated. Gabriel needs us. He has to live with this condition. He cannot help himself.

We put everything aside. We will do what my youngest son Loren, told us:

- Mom, this is the child we will have to help and teach. He is that way and all that remains is for us to do the most we can for him.

True. Gabriel is an angel.

Thank You, God, for this special child. Thanks for letting us be here to help him. Thanks for granting us the understanding of his condition, for us having the guidance to look for solutions and for helping. Above all, thanks because we have hope.

Notes

CHAPTER 3

LIFE GOES ON

After this storm there came a period of time in which my daughter and I faced what would be a constant struggle against the condition that wanted to take Gabriel away from us. Life goes on. Everyone returned to their chores and routines.

I realized that all had been already provided by God, our Supreme Maker. Before all this occurred, I had decided to retire early. I had intended to write a book, (obviously not this one), take care of my ailing mother, and enjoy, while still fairly young, a time of rest and relaxation. What irony!

After the diagnosis all kinds of exams followed. The first one was a scan of his little brain to eliminate the possibilities of tumors or deficiencies. They gave him a sedative to allow them to place all the leads. It was very difficult since Gabriel struggled against anything that would touch his head. We distracted him with a toy that still interests him today. It simulates a CD player that includes a disc with a spiral drawing that appears to revolve increasing its size and is accompanied by different music alternatives and a screen with a sequence that repeats itself constantly. It cost us only ten dollars. We have not found it since. He did not fall asleep until all the cables had been put on him.

That was followed by a blood test, again with his favorite toy. It went a lot better since the nurse was skillful enough to prick him correctly the first time and did it in such a manner so that Gabriel did not see the needle. May God bless her!

The MRI was traumatic since the sedative did not take effect immediately. He fell asleep in his father's arms, but when he laid him down on the stretcher, Gabriel woke up. They had to double the dosage and he finally fell asleep in my arms. Afterwards, we had to wake him up to make sure that he would awaken in a safe period of time.

While I was waiting I prayed deeply and I had a vision. In my vision there were Gabriel and four other children surrounding Our Lord Jesus Christ, who was seated while the children were standing. The Lord instructed Gabriel to go into the world. Gabriel looked at Him as if asking him for his blessings and Jesus approved. Gabriel came to us. Gabriel was sent by the Lord, and he was again our angel.

He awakened. It was already noon and he had not eaten anything.

At the same time as they were doing the studies they cauterized some warts that appeared on his face and arms. Every trip to the doctor was like a return journey since Gabriel already knew the road travelled to the dermatologist.

We started speech therapy, ABA and occupational therapy. At first Gabriel went like a zombie, but soon he learned that there he was required to do some activities. On one occasion we had to return without therapy, because he started to scream desperately, he threw himself down at the entrance and the therapist told me that in that condition they would not accomplish anything. Today, I thank her because I know that when he is pushed too much it upsets his nervous system even more.

-All of this is for your good, my love. Grandma is here. I will not leave you unless God takes me away from your side. You are not alone. Mom is here.

Notes

Notes

CHAPTER 4

THE DIET

In November I went to see my mother in Puerto Rico. While she and my dad were lying down I told them:

> - Mom, I could not come for your birthday because they were doing some tests on Gabriel and found him to be autistic.
>
> - What is that? - she asked after a while, in her characteristically humble way.
>
> - Well...that his brain does not function well.

My mother cried. I still feel her sobs in my heart. It was the last time we cried together.

When I returned I found Gabriel very peaceful. He looked at me and then continued watching television from up close. He was not agitated, nothing seemed to hurt him. My daughter gave me the news. She found information on the internet about diets for autistic children. Gabriel had not had any milk for a week and had improved a lot. I read all that she had printed out for me. Milk has a protein called 'casein' that has the same effect as opium on these children. We decided to change him to soy milk, but Gabriel started to spin again, shaking his hands and looking at the walls sideways while walking. We later learned that soy milk does not have casein but that the molecular composition of soy is similar to cow's milk and the bodies of some children do not distinguish between the two and have the same reaction to both. We decided to give him rice milk.

While doing research, my daughter found the testimony of a mother who was able to arrest the physical as well as mental deterioration of her autistic child. We bought her book "Special Diets for Special Kids" by Lisa Lewis. She recommends a series of laboratory tests to determine what she calls 'intolerance', rather than allergy to 'gluten', another versatile protein that is found this time in wheat flour. This protein is able to penetrate the weakened intestinal walls and enter the blood stream till it reaches the cerebral membrane and alters the brain functions.

The days that followed the diagnosis and tests were exhausting for Gabriel. The minute we would go into the car, he would become nervous. Every day there was something new. It was possibly for this reason, or because we were better informed, that we noticed a dramatic deterioration in his health and coordination. What most worried us was his spinning while looking at the ceiling, shaking his little hands, walking while looking at the wall and bending his toes backwards as if walking on a stump. Dreadful! We were intrigued. What is happening to him? We started to study the condition and gather additional information in order to take a road, a direction that would enable us to effectively help our child.

We received a call from Kenia, the babysitter who used to take care of him.

> - Mom, I know a lady who has a granddaughter who was diagnosed with autism and did not speak. They took her to this doctor and, in less than a year, the little girl began to improve. Now no one could quiet her down.
>
> - Who is this doctor? , I said in disbelief.

- His office is in Aventura, he is a doctor in alternative 'natural' medicine.

- Is he accredited?

- I don't know, but I have her telephone number, you have nothing to loose by inquiring.

- Very well, thanks.

She gave me the telephone number, not before telling me that she was organizing a group of people to pray for Gabriel.

-Thanks for your love and for the tender and patient way you took care of our baby!

We called the lady, she gave us the information and we made an appointment with this doctor, which was to be in two months.

While waiting for the appointed time we continued looking for information. It was all frustrating. There is no cure. The cause is unknown. There is no recovery. One out of every 150 children in the United States is autistic. My God! We are facing a plague. How is it possible that no one with sufficient power has raised their voice in complaint? Why has no one publicized this? And, if it is publicized, why doesn't anyone listen or give it the importance it deserves? What is the government doing, the agencies that supposedly represent the public interests? We are talking about our children. Why don't they educate the parents? What special interests are involved in all this? Now, I clearly understand the chapter in which Don Quijote confronts some windmills thinking they are giants.

I am not giving up, I am going to fight, even if in my attempt all goes wrong, even if I feel alone, even if the giant throws me down a million times, I will get up. Gabriel needs me. All those children abandoned by those responsible for investigating their situation, need it. The parents, at the mercy of ignorance, need it.

CHAPTER 5

THE CRISIS

We made the mistake of implementing the diet and removing the gluten from his diet all at once. It was too drastic, a decision based on despair and determination to do something to help the child. It had the same effect as when an addict tries to break the habit. We should have done it slowly, we found this out later on, but it was already done, and we could not turn back. As his body was requiring gluten he became delirious. Lights terrorized him. He cried uncontrollably. He got chills and turned yellowish, a disturbing and moving picture. There were many times when I, desperately, would hug a column in the kitchen and sob out of the feeling of uselessness. During the day Gabriel did not coordinate his movements and would bump into door knobs, and at night the crisis would intensify. He seemed to be looking for or running away from something.

- Grandpa, let's take Gabriel for a ride in the car and see if he will calm down.

- Now? It is ten o'clock at night. It is very late. He might catch a cold. He is hungry or he misses his mother.

- Let's go…maybe it will comfort him.

I wrapped him in a blanket and went out. This went on every night. When his mother returned from college, she would find us watching television, eating potato chips or rice cakes.

A few weeks later Gabriel started to 'wake up'. We attended his therapies without major problems. Generally, on the way, I used to take him to the playground so he would associate the therapy with something pleasant. I had to help him climb because he did not have the strength in his muscles. It was as if his joints were made of rags and were not put together. He would lie down without strength when he got to the top. At other times he would get dizzy. He started to look up at the sky when he was coming down the slide and constantly repeated the phoneme 'gggggg' or 'ttttt.'

I remember one day a little boy looked at him and made a gesture to his friend pointing to his ear meaning that he was crazy. This, far from upsetting, since he was just a child, made me think about what was awaiting Gabriel when he would attend school. What would happen to him? How would he react to criticism, to rejection?

He continued to improve and show signs of pain, but he did not utter words, nor syllables, and his daze continued to be lost.

At Christmas my son, Loren, paid us a visit with his children. They are compassionate and understanding children. Loren tried to play with him throwing him up in the air.

> - Mom, this is the way he is. Even if he enjoys it he does not show it.

Far from reassuring myself of his well being, Gabriel's lack of expression alarmed me.

In occupational therapy they recommended this book to me: "The Out- of-Sync Child". It helped me to design activities to strengthen his muscles. His grandfather made him a fort with a swing,' Teeter-Tooter' something like a see-saw on the ground for him to walk on that would force him to balance his body, and a rope ladder to climb on. Every day we dedicated some time to exercise his muscles and coordination. Sometimes, I had to excuse myself with parents in the playground, because he would bump into the children and did not notice them, as if he did not see them.

He continued with therapy till the month of July of the following year, when he was transferred to a school for autistic children, supposedly the best in the area. We thought we were blessed.

Notes

Notes

CHAPTER 6

MEDICAL ATTENTION

The day of the medical appointment arrived. We had already made the pertinent inquiries about his credentials and certificates. 'Traditional' medical doctors apparently do no not approve of natural or alternative treatments, but they do not offer anything different in exchange, only the therapies. There is no proven treatment available that will effectively and permanently help autistic children. We already have therapies but Gabriel is still absent. We need to attack the causes for this condition, seek a way to help him. We know something hurts him, especially before having a bowel movement. He has no strength, makes stigmatic gestures, and does not communicate at all.

The doctor's humble demeanor surprised us, given his recognition. He asked us questions, which opened our eyes to a world of new worries and questions. His poor digestive system immediately stood out. Questions related to his vaccines and his weak immune system...what a surprise!

He would perform specialized laboratory tests. Immediately, he would help him completely digest foods with enzymes. His immune system would be strengthened with 'Colostrum' and his intestines with cod fish oil among other things. He recommended some baths with Epsom salt and a cream of Epsom salt, which gave him incredible relief. There were other supplements like Taurine, Glycine, Culturelle, Folinic Acid, Nuthera, and others that we administered to him gradually.

Administering all these medications to a child 30 months old is worrisome, especially if there are doctors that consistently reject them. It is not a decision made lightly, not without certain reservations, but Gabriel's nervous system, his motor skills as well as his intelligence plummeted.

A Gabriel who we did not know, emerged from the crisis following the diagnosis, one who did not even recognize his own mother, he would take the hand of any stranger to help him, locked in a world that we had no access to, but in which, we knew he felt lost by his tears. We could not leave him to chance. The therapies and diet had helped him a lot, but his 'absence', his lack of contact with those who surrounded him and his debilitated physical stability gave indication that something was not functioning.

I turned to may Pastor's wife.

> - Glorita, I do not know what to do. I have a lot of faith in the Lord, but I believe that God expects me to take steps, to demonstrate my confidence, and not remain with folded arms, without taking action.

> - Pray, pray a lot. Every time you give him medicine, ask God that He should be the one at work that the medicine will help him get better.

I have not stopped praying, the more demanding the situation, the more I come to Our God. My hope rests in Him. We do what is humanly possible.

We returned to the doctor's office after approximately a month.

> - The child has a bacteria in his intestines called 'Clostridia'. This bacteria releases some toxins that, when they get to the brain produce delirium

and hallucinations. He also has a bacteria in his urine known as 'yeast'.

- Can that be cured?

- We will prescribe him Nystatin for the yeast; it is a medication for fungus. The 'clostridia' will be controlled with Culturelle.

We have to attack both conditions at the same time, one controls the other. If only one is treated, the other will take over.

I received a call from my daughter in law, Keyla:

- Mom, do you know that my little neighbor who you know is autistic?

- Really? He does not appear to be.

- Yes, I had noticed strange things, but I did not know…

- Don't you know what they did to help him talk?

- Yes, they told me that they spent a fortune on his treatment, but that they received a lot of help from a book that they are going to send you.

- Really!

- His father is a Pastor, what a coincidence!

- Oh, thanks. May God bless them.

It is not a coincidence. It is God answering our prayers. Today, this book, "Biological Treatments for Autism and PDD" by Dr. Shaw, PHD is immensely informative and I have received guidance that has been a determining factor in Gabriel's progress. We do not have all the financial means necessary to attack this evil, but God provides us with the ways to receive, although in a limited way, the help we need. Thanks, my Lord; because we are not alone; "My grace is sufficient for you, for power is made perfect in weakness." (2 Cor 12:9)

Notes

CHAPTER 7

GABRIEL

We already had therapy sessions for Gabriel, we had established his diet and he had medical supervision. It is a question of putting it all into action and awaiting his reaction.

Everything was going so slowly! I was in charge of preparing his foods and taking him to his therapy sessions daily. I tried to keep him entertained at all times, but it was impossible. I took him to the playground almost every day. My husband and daughter would come home at night.

Gabriel is an extremely passive child. He does not have temper tantrums and he is submissive. He still hurts when he sits on the toilet. He does his needs leaning to one side.

He has, nevertheless, an unexplainable characteristic, an inclination to approach certain people who specifically call his attention. For example, one day, while he was on the swings, he saw from afar a lady who was alone and seated on a park bench. He came down from the fort and went to where the lady was. I followed him closely but I could not avoid his approaching her and tapping her on the shoulders.

-I am sorry, he is autistic- I said apologizing.

- It doesn't matter, he brightened up my day.

My mother passed away in May, before Gabriel started school.Although I had traveled to Puerto Rico during her grave illness, I was unable to be there during the last two weeks prior to her death. Cindy, Gabriel's mom, had finished her studies and had a good job. Her boss, an exceptionally understanding person, had allowed her to be absent, but it became too much. Because my daughter is a single mother, Gabriel receives visitations from his father once a week or once every two weeks. I had to stay with Gabriel during the day.

My mother, who was 86 years old, always told me that she wanted me to accompany her at the moment of death, but it was not to be, at least not physically. My soul trembled anxiously when I received the news at dawn.

I told Cindy early in the morning:

- Mom passed away.

- Oh, mom, I am sorry.

We embraced each other and cried. I had planned to return home that Wednesday and she died on Tuesday.

Later during therapy, I told the therapist:

- I don't know what is wrong with Gabriel. He is having a bad day. I don't know if he knows that I am sad. My mother died and I told Cindy in front of him.

- One has to be careful with these children. They are very sensitive. When I am depressed, I prefer not to work with them because they are aware of it.

That is how Gabriel, my angel, is. May God help and strengthen him. He will need a lot of support in order to face so much rejection and criticism in this society!

In the summer we went to Puerto Rico. My father, who was the same age as my mother, now alone, wanted to meet his great grandchild. From the time that he found out about his condition, he made an effort to help Gabriel as well as Cindy, offering them his unconditional support.

The fresh beach air did him well. My siblings and close relatives met him.

My brother, who is a police officer, entered the house one day and full of sorrow, said to me:

> - I killed a guy.
>
> - My God! What happened?
>
> - He was firing at me during a robbery and I hit him with the police car.
>
> - Oh God!

We hugged each other. I did not know what to say. My brother went into the living room and sat down on the sofa and put his head in his hands. Gabriel walked around the dining room, went to my brother and patted him on his back.

The night before our return, our Pastor Arnaldo, Glorita, and her mother came to visit us. The six of us made a prayer circle, since my father had gone to bed. The Pastor ended the prayer saying:

> - Lord, we ask you for a miracle!

Yes, we hope for a miracle, a miracle of love, a miracle of faith.

Notes

Notes

CHAPTER 8

THERAPIES

Gabriel was to start school at the age of 3 years and 2 months. The therapy offered by the government in the "Child Development Center" extended to the summer. A year had already gone by! Gabriel did not qualify for more.

The teachers visited our home to meet Gabriel. He looked at them attentively with certain reservation. We informed them of his diet, his medications, and his personality.

> -He has progressed a lot. He no longer repeats phonemes incessantly and recognizes the people close to us. He adores his mother and showers her with kisses and hugs. He is tender and loving. He does not have temper tantrums; he is extremely passive and submissive.

We informed them what he could eat and drink. We insisted on the dangers of the hidden gluten in paint, glue and wax that covers books. We will give him his medications before he goes to school. I would go later to administer to him his enzyme before lunch.

In the months prior to the beginning of school we intensified his speech therapy. My daughter contracted a therapist through the internet. He had two, hour long sessions twice a week at our home. Although it seems like a lot, it wasn't because out of this time, the therapist would take time out to plan activities upon her arrival, and would give him recess in between during which time she would take notes again. During recess Gabriel would come running out of his room and hug me.

All was going well till one day when the mailman arrived and he rang the doorbell. I picked up the package and closed the door when I heard Gabriel crying. Upon entering the room the scene I observed worried me greatly. Apparently, Gabriel thought that it was his mother who had arrived and he was struggling to get out and welcome her. When I entered, the therapist was holding him down with one hand on his shoulders and her knee against his chest to keep him in place, while with her forefinger she was showing him the movement of the lips in order to make sounds. I told her:

- It appears that he thinks that his mother has arrived.

I took Gabriel away from her and turned him upside down in order to allow him to calm himself. Once he was calm, Gabriel returned to the room and completed his session. I told my daughter what had happened. When my husband paid her and told her not to return she commented:

- He knows more than you think.

Of course he knows a lot, but he was not always like this! Gabriel has suffered quite a bit with his condition and we struggle with him to overcome it. We do not need to pay someone to jeopardize his progress.

When I commented what had happened to the therapists from the Center they recommended a therapist familiar with the field. She would give him therapy in the office, but unfortunately after a couple sessions she was injured. She recommended one of her students and we started all over again.

Due to the difficulty in brushing Gabriel's teeth, since he does not open his mouth because of his great sensitivity, we decided to take him to the dentist for a cleaning. The dentist said that he needed some extractions, fillings and crowns. It was not surprising to us since we had already noticed indications of cavities. He told us that rice milk promotes decay, but it is the only one he tolerates. We decided not to give him anything besides water, to avoid sugars, when putting him to bed.

Notes

Notes

CHAPTER 9

THE SCHOOL

In the midst of all these conditions we started the new school year. Gabriel was to begin a new phase in his life.

Three years old and we had to leave him in front of the building! Any teacher would receive him. Had he been a 'normal' child, I would have understood. Parents were to approach in their cars. They could not get out and someone would come to pick the children up. How afraid some of them were!

By that time we were giving him Culturelle, Colostrum, Cod fish oil, Super Nuthera, Folinic Acid, Glycine, Taurine and enzymes before breakfast. After that the ride to school took at least 45 minutes. Often Gabriel got nauseous and threw up before arriving. I stopped, changed him and kept on going. I did volunteer to work there in order to be available in case they needed me.

Gabriel continued improving. He looked at us more consciously. There was a goldfish tank at the exit of the school which always caught his attention. I usually stopped and allowed him to look at it since I signed him out before dismissal. Otherwise I had to expose him to the same process as in the morning.

Because he vomited so much in the morning, the principal agreed to let me bring him a little later. This way I accompanied him inside and I assured him that I would wait for him. I often remained at the school.

The first week he got hit on his back at the level of his kidneys. We were greatly worried because the bruise was large. My daughter requested to talk to the teacher. She did not know how he got hurt.

-It did not seem to hurt him because he did not cry.

Any special education professional knows about the lack of feeling or expression of autistic children.

On one occasion when a few students were absent because of an upcoming holiday, I asked the teacher if I could take him home with me. She answered me that he was fine. I waited a few hours, but decided to take him with me.

- Where is Gabriel?

- Oh, he is in the other classroom with the other children of his age.

I went to look for him. He was sitting in a little rocking chair.

- Gabriel, Gabriel, here is grandma.

There was no reaction.

- He loves that chair- the teacher said.

I took him with me to the car.

- Hey, Gabriel, what is wrong?

He started to regress. He most likely ingested gluten. The following Monday, I went to the principal.

- I would like to talk to the teacher because somehow Gabriel ate something harmful.

She called the teacher.

- Is Gabriel putting books covered with wax, play dough, glue or something to that nature, in his mouth? - I asked.

-No, I haven't noticed anything.

-Do those things contain gluten?

-Yes, and other things like fish food.

-I understand about fish food…

-Yes, I am very worried because gluten remains in the system from six to nine months.

-That long?

I felt like bringing her some literature, but she already had the information. Isn't it assumed that they are knowledgeable in the field, at least, informed?

A few days later the assistant told me:

- Last week the director came to class and she gave Gabriel cheerios every time he did what she would ask him to do. I told her that she should not do this because of his diet.

- A lot?

- No, about 5 or 6.

That same assistant had told me that Gabriel was weak because of his diet. I did not know what to think.

Being a volunteer I witnessed something that even today, with all my studies and experience, I have not been able to justify. A teacher was holding on her lap a little boy, about ten years old, disabling him with her arm around his chest. With her other hand she was opening his mouth. Another teacher was putting pieces of banana in his mouth and shutting his mouth. The little boy was choking, but swallowed.

I asked myself if this is what they did to Gabriel the day that he did not want to eat lunch and I told them that I would have to take him home to feed him since I had already given him the enzyme.

- I thought that you said, in your note, that it did not matter.

- No! He has to eat something. I gave him the enzyme.

They removed him from the cafeteria and took him to the room since they did not want him to see me. A little while later the occupational therapist informed me:

- He ate all of his food.

In the afternoon the assistant told me:

- Gabriel said 'go' for me.

- Yes? How is that?

- When he finished eating I told him that if he did not say 'go' he was not going, and he said it.

I was surprised, but my surprise was even greater when that afternoon Gabriel arrived at the car and I noticed broken capillaries in his cheeks.

The incidents worsened and one day, as I was leaving I heard Gabriel crying loudly. I approached the hallway, and heard the assistant screaming at him:

- No! No!

He was coming out of the bathroom full of tears and red. Her face was contorted. I asked what had happened.

- I tried to seat him on the toilet and he was kicking me, so I held him down firmly.

Gabriel's intestines hurt him and she knows it.

My angel, how much you must have gone through, and I not knowing about it! How many times must you have wanted to scream, 'grandma, I want to go home!' And I was so close to you!

Not all parents of autistic children are able to pay for private therapy sessions, not all are understood in their home. In this entire dilemma there is so much pain, so much insensitivity, so much ignorance.

I voiced my concerns to both my husband and my daughter.

- Mom, don't meddle. Just take care of Gabriel.

- He needs to learn and go to school.

I know that Gabriel is my grandchild, my blood, but I hurt for all autistic children, they are my civic responsibility, my moral duty. I can't just cross my arms and look away.

A few days later I came to a decision.

- I need to speak to the Director.

- She is not in today. Can it be tomorrow at 10 A.M.?

- Of course.

The next day before lunch, I met with the Director.

- I am coming to you because the first time we brought Gabriel to see the school we went to the playground. All the teachers were gathered together talking and the children were playing. When they saw you, they got up and went to look after the children.

- Yes, because they know that it is their duty to attend to them. (She smiled)

- Do you know that they bit Gabriel yesterday?

- They beat or bit him?

- They bit him (I accepted the correction of my pronunciation) the teacher did not even notice the bite. I turned back from the car and brought him to her so she could see it. She didn't know about it.

- We already know who did it and we are taking care of this.

- Another thing; when we returned from Christmas vacation, Gabriel cried a lot. I asked the Occupational therapist when she came out of the room, what was the matter with him, and she told me that it was not Gabriel, but another child who did not want to work. When we arrived home and I took off his shoes, they had left on his socks a piece of sawdust from the playground stuck to it and as he was walking it dug into his nail. That was the reason he did not want to work. They should pay more attention and look for the reasons why the children cry.

She winced.

- You can be my eyes and ears. I cannot be in all places. What else have you noticed?

I found the suggestion strange since on the day mentioned she was in a meeting with the Principal in the office next door with the door open. When I approached the room where Gabriel was, they shut the door avoiding my intrusion. I recounted the memory and said:

> - Well, I think that the educational philosophy, the way in which you try to change the children's behavior is not the most appropriate way.

> - What are you referring to?

> - Don't you think that locking a child up in the bathroom is a bit drastic?

> - I know which child you are talking about, and it is not that we lock him up in the bathroom. It is that every time he wants attention he vomits and we are trying to change his behavior.

> - Locking him up in the bathroom while he is screaming "I'm done", is that a good way?

> - We will try to find other ways. Thanks anyway, I will take action.

She understood. I did not need to tell her anymore, she already knew.

The next day they have the same child locked up in a little conference room.

> - That child's screams breaks my heart. I think about how the parents of this child would react if they find themselves in this situation.

A mother who was there, answered with her back to me:

>-That child is new and they are teaching him the rules.

> - New? I have been here since the beginning of the year and that child has been here for more than a month.

There was silence. Another mother who was present was speechless.

> - I am leaving, said the previous one, and she left the place.

What is good for one is good for all, I thought. God, look after all the children who even with their parents are abandoned, whether it is because of a lack of knowledge, because there is no alternative, or because of inertia.

The culminating point that marked Gabriel's departure from that school arrived before I was able to change my husband's and daughter's opinion about the consequences of leaving him there. They insisted that the child had to attend, no matter how much he was exposed to. They thought that these were 'grandma issues', a very typical attitude when it comes to me.

One day when we went to pick him up early, I said to my daughter in the car:

- Look, observe objectively from here, how they treat them.

We saw how a teacher was holding a child between her legs trying to prevent him from playing. Another one did not allow a little girl to ride the battery operated car and she got in it.

One child left the group and the teacher brought him back holding him so tightly by the arm that one could observe his gesture of pain.

- This is like a boot camp!

To my understanding pushing them too hard exposes their nervous system to get more tangled up, lowers their self-esteem, if they have any, and increases their confusion about the social environment.

I taught for 38 years and I know there is a big difference between teaching and training. If you force children to do something as if they were little dogs who had to obey, you do not increase under any circumstance, the absorbing availability or capability of the child. He does things like a zombie not like a thinking being. I believe that autistic children have the ability to learn be it to a greater or lesser degree. You should teach them by example, one follows a sequence with a final goal in mind, you reward their effort, you teach them the satisfaction of completing an activity. You show them how to eat a banana. You teach them how to let you know they are going to throw up, through signals or gestures made to their caregiver, whatever the need.

Through instruction, the behavior becomes an intrinsic part of them, through training, they obey methodically without thinking.

On that fateful day the teacher who was in charge was not in school. Only the assistant and a substitute teacher were there. Truthfully, I do not know how Gabriel got a hold of a package of Oreo cookies. He had already learned that what is not on his plate is not his, much less to take something from another child. The sad part is that he ate them.

When we arrived in the afternoon to pick him up the assistant called me into the room and the Principal followed me.

> - He had a reaction. He could not control himself, but he is fine now. We took him outside for a walk.

- Why didn't you call me?

- He is fine now.

Gabriel was seated with the other children, moving his little body back and forth. He did not see me. He did not know that I was there. The Principal turned around and left the room without saying a word. I was dismayed. I took him to his mother.

- He ate some Oreo cookies, - I told her.

- Gabriel, Gabriel, sweetheart, it's mommy.

There was no reaction. His gaze was lost. My daughter drove home.

- Why did you eat that, dear? You knew that it was not yours. You have wanted it for a long time, right? You were just waiting for the right moment. Aha!

We laughed nervously and hugged him. We did not know what was awaiting us. A year and a half of progress went tumbling down!

We did not receive even one phone call from the school during the following two weeks, nor ever. Not how it happened, not why they had not called us right away, not even "we are sorry, it was an accident". We did not hear anything. Even though it would not have made any difference, it would have been encouraging. Knowing that someone is concerned helps a lot.

Notes

Notes

CHAPTER 10

REGRESSION

We called the doctor the same day the incident occurred. He recommended to us that we should immediately give him an enzyme to help him digest the gluten, DPP IV. We also gave him baking soda every four hours to clean out his intestines. Unfortunately, almost six hours had gone by when we arrived home and reached the doctor.

The next day Gabriel was walking on the stumps of his feet, looking at the walls as he was walking, mesmerized by the lights, etc. My big question at that time was if he had reached the point of no return, which Lisa Lewis cites of in her book. What an agony!

From the time that we started the treatment I kept a diary in which I kept track of what Gabriel ate and the reactions to each food. This way I could accurately point to his reactions to each food. The later entries to the ingestion of gluten could not be more explicit:

On Thursday, March 16th they gave him gluten in school. They did not call me. When I went to pick him up, he was sitting spaced out making the sounds (ggggg).

He did not get up when he saw me. He did not have a happy expression or anything. I took him to the car. He did not notice Cindy. He became very sick when we arrived. He became limp, and he did not want to get up from the floor. He was kicking Cindy.

He is not reacting to language. He seems to be gone. He does not know what is happening to him.

He fell asleep within the hour, at 3 o'clock, after we took him for a ride for a little while.

The doctor told us to give him baking soda. We also gave him vitamin C.

Friday the 17th

He walked on the tip of his toes. He is not very alert but he did his physical therapy on Monday. A friend of mine came with her grandson and another little girl. We went to the park.

On Saturday and Sunday he was very quiet, isolated.

Monday the 20th

He had therapy, he continues to gaze as if looking through someone, isolated.

Tuesday the 21st

I gave him papaya in order for him to eliminate the gluten faster.

Wednesday the 22nd

He is looking at the walls and turning objects around. His hands are limp and he holds them in front of his chest. They are hurting him.

We knew that the stimulating effect of casein is gradually eliminated in approximately three days, but the gluten would remain in his body for quite a while.

All that was left for us to do was to pray, pray, pray and hope.

-Yes, "your power strengthens in weakness"- I repeated to myself.

- My God, I trust in You.

The regression that Gabriel experienced was painful. We started to attempt to help him to cleanse his system once more. Ironically, we were happy we knew what we were supposed to do. Bécquer says;

"In my sadness I have some happiness; is that and I still have tears".[my translation]

We know the healing effect of garlic, cilantro or oregano on the intestines. All his foods contained them, and Epsom Salt to provide him with additional sulfates to defend himself from the toxins in his bath.

We increased the hours of the ABA therapist in order to keep him up to date with the skills he was supposedly getting in school, and we hired a speech therapist who we previously knew from the Center and who worked in the school Gabriel had attended.

The one who gave ABA went to some conferences where they discussed things that aggravate autism and they referred to several books. When she arrived at my house she commented to me about an aspect I had not contemplated and it had to do with the environment.

When I studied the book "In Harm's Way: Toxic Threats to Child Development", published by Greater Boston Physicians for Social Responsibility, a whole new range of aspects to consider opened in front of me and my hope was renewed.

Some people, who I trusted, distanced themselves because of the situation. We received confusing and poor interpretations from those who did not understand our restlessness and dedication to Gabriel. From the ones I trusted most, some abandoned us, and others kept their distance not knowing how to react or approach us. Others, without knowing, gave me the support I needed. The people who saw Gabriel before the treatment noticed the difference. A mother, whose child had shared one of Gabriel's first therapy sessions with him, visited the school prior to the incident and commented to the teacher:

- Is that Gabriel? I know that child! What a difference!

We had to return to that point and improve since something else had to be taken care of.

Before Gabriel left the school we had started the process of fixing his teeth. We took him on an empty stomach. They gave him a sedative and we left the office to wait for it to take effect. He did not fall asleep till we returned 45 minutes later. He fell asleep as he was passing the door. Thank God, I said to myself.

While I was waiting I called my father. Since my mother passed away, a few months prior, I used to call to let him know about Gabriel.

-Dad, I am at the dentist's office. They put Gabriel to sleep because they are going to do some extractions. He has 14 cavities! Afterwards they are going to do other things to him.

-Tell me when he comes out and how he is.

I called him in the afternoon.

- Oh, Dad, what a picture! When they called us they had not yet awakened him. They wanted Cindy to be there when he woke up. They had him tied up with straps, an apparatus to keep his mouth opened and Gabriel was covered with blood. I almost fainted.

- Poor thing, and how about his mother?

- Well, you know she keeps quiet.

- Take care of her as well.

-Yes, dad, don't worry.

These were my constant conversations with Dad. He was always as worried about his daughter, as his granddaughter, and his grandson.

The whole dental process took about 3 to 4 months. At the end Gabriel already knew the way and did not want to enter upon arrival. These are one of those things one does out of necessity and not for him to be content with the process.

In the research that was published in the aforementioned book, it is concluded that the contamination in the environment prevails and causes poor absorption in some children. One example is carbon monoxide. Not everyone reacts the same way to its exposure. To this, add pesticides that are airborne and the smoke that comes from different sources including barbecues, cigarettes, emissions from equipment, and thousands of contaminants having damaging effects.

As if this was not enough, add to this detergents and disinfectants used in the home, that enter the body through the skin or the nose and overload the deficient immune system of children like Gabriel.

We avoided giving him 'phenols' in his nutrition, but at the same time he is exposed to the invasion of all these chemicals which, in certain ways, are inevitable in the environment in which we live. Even going for a walk is dangerous for him! How do we avoid this!

As if this was not enough, there is the aggravation of pesticides, insecticides, medications and hormones with which they treat farming and animals, which makes food a sword with a double edge.

As I was reviewing the tests that the doctor had prescribed for Gabriel, after a few months on Nystatin, I was surprised to see a note from the laboratory which indicated the presence of a detergent used in job areas. I was flabbergasted. Gabriel had never ingested anything like that. I called Kenya and told her.

-No, mom, no. When the lady cleaned I used to watch Gabriel.

I then thought about the trip we took during the hurricane when Gabriel licked the floor. Numerous ideas were pounding in my head.

How it happened, is already in the past. Besides, that by itself does not create autism; it is another aggravating factor. We cannot lock him up in a bubble. This is the world he has to live in.

By then, we had decided to do the first 'chelation' to see if he would eliminate metals and toxins. We had to travel to Tampa. At the same time they also gave him blood tests. We returned the same day to Palm Beach, stopping to collect urine samples. It was exhausting for Gabriel who had been exposed to these procedures and was weak.

We started the process of incorporating an organic diet in conjunction with organic detergents and avoiding, as much as possible, the contaminants of the environment, including the water he drinks.

One day, in the playground, a worker with a sprayer or exterminating container, approaching us, started to spray pesticide.

- Wait, wait! Let me take the child away.

- This will not do anything to him- and he continued.

- Yes, it does. It affects his nervous system!

Some of the spray fell on his little legs. I took Gabriel in my arms and ran out. I went home and ran water over his legs for a while. I imagine that the man thought that I was a hypochondriac, but I did not care! I felt like putting the container on his head, as a hat.

There are many like this, who do not understand this condition. They do as much as they can but come to feel it is useless and it is madness. We received comments from teachers and even from a pediatrician who told us:

- Someone is robbing you of your money.

Do you know what? I will do anything I can. Where there is genuine hope, I will go. And as far as the money is concerned, God will provide.

> "All that is in your hands to do, do according to your strength because in the tomb, where you will go, there is no labor, no work..." Ecclesiastes 9:10

How lonely we felt at times! What a sensation of uselessness and uncertainty! What lack of understanding! What ignorance! From the worker who cleans to the pediatrician who treats him... Even the teachers who 'teach' him. Where do we go from here? There we were, my daughter and I, holding Gabriel by the hand, facing a labyrinth, and we did not know which would be the best option for him, or even if there was an option...

Notes

Notes

CHAPTER 11

THE NEW SCHOOL

During the summer months Gabriel continued with his therapy sessions at home. We established a pattern of daily activities for him that included trips to the park, visits to the mall, time at the beach and exercises in the patio. His biggest attraction was television, even though he loved the beach. We bought him a swimming pool, about 10'in diameter and that is where he spent most of the time. When his obsession with television became uncontrollable we decided to buy him a DVD player in order to diminish the emissions from the television waves and the electromagnetic field. The DVD player became his favorite toy. He ate, played and slept with it. He learned to maneuver it at will, and did not accept anything else but his DVD player. Many people told us to take it away from him but then he isolated himself more. We opted to allow him to have the DVD player and we bought him educational DVD's, including Baby Bumble Bee for him to communicate, and others.

The therapist started to use it as a reward and so did we. At least his obsession was not that repetitive since we redirected it toward something constructive. The obsessive character of autistic children is one of the biggest problems to solve.

At any rate our greatest responsibility is to make Gabriel a happy child. Whether his autistic condition is irreversible or not, our objective is for him to learn to live with whatever is available to him. To submit him to criticism and intolerance, a product of mediocrity, is not part of our agenda.

My daughter researched the new school before making a decision. She put Gabriel on the waiting list of 'Bauduin Preschool', a much sought school for autistic children. She moved close to the school hoping and waiting for him to be accepted. On the day that we received the news that he had been accepted, we thanked God.

When I visited the school for the first time I was impressed by the professional atmosphere and the diligence with which they did their work. I was not expecting such quality, especially since it was a non-profit organization. Few parents have access to a school that combines good educational quality with understanding and dedication.

Gabriel adapted immediately to his 'routine'. He would put his backpack in the cubby and his lunch in a basket. After that, he would go to his table, sit down in his little chair where a transitional exercise awaited him. He would remove the fastener from his cards, pull it apart and place it in separate containers. He would place the cards in front of him and wait for the teacher, ready to start the day. There were six little boys, one teacher and two assistants in his class.

At the beginning, Gabriel was not totally free from the gluten, which is why he would keep walking along the large classroom windows. I made a comment to the teacher about our desire to toilet train him. She insisted that we wait, because in her opinion, he was not ready. I thanked her for her judgment on that occasion and many others.

When Gabriel arrived home he would throw himself on the floor and could hardly climb up the stairs to the second floor. I was very worried about his weakness and the weakness in his joints; it was as if he had been intoxicated.

Notes

Notes

CHAPTER 12

THE BEGINNING OF RECUPERATION

Because the trip to Tampa was so difficult, we decided to take him to a new doctor, this time in Miami. We signed him out every time he had an appointment. The teacher always inquired about the treatment and observed him.

The new doctor immediately added supplements to the list among others, Zinc of which his level was below normal, given its properties to help him process proteins. He kept the others, Nystatin being one of them. He suggested that we start him immediately on a series of 'chelations' to get rid of the metals and toxins in his body.

From the recommendations of the previous doctor my daughter investigated the benefits of the hyperbaric chamber. We thought that if it was not going to eliminate his autism at least it would help his brain. The new doctor recommended this to us as well, which is why we started him on a combination of 'chelations' and the treatment. He had 10 sessions of these oxygenations which he enjoyed since he always took along his DVD player.

When the first results of the bacteria in his intestines came (Clostridia) the doctor prescribed Vancomycin for a month. During the treatment I was skeptical since Gabriel started to get sick more often, especially after the 'chelations'.

The trips to Miami lasted almost the entire first semester of school. My daughter would arrive quickly from her job in Boca Raton to pick us up so we could immediately leave for Miami. We used to return about 6 P.M., with luck, due to the traffic at that hour. Sometimes, on the way, we had to collect urine for testing. There were times when Gabriel lost three or four days of school.

By January, Gabriel was already four and a half years old, and we started to notice improvement in his concentration, disposition, motor skills and his integration into the family unit. Little by little, things started to normalize and Gabriel became stronger.

In March, my father passed away. It was devastating for me because I felt that I had not spent enough time with him during his last days. He was 87 years old. He was unable to overcome my mother's death. We saw him loose his will to live and never recuperated his strength after her illness and absence. Loneliness killed him, loneliness of the soul, loneliness of his being, loneliness of his spirit. Since he found out about Gabriel's diagnosis his constant recommendation to us was that we should shower him with love and attention. He ended each conversation with: "Take care of Cindy". Today I know that he understood my absence.

One day, I took Gabriel to his pediatrician for one of his constant colds accompanied by a fever, and I was surprised to see how Gabriel waited to be called in. He did not give any signs of confusion or uncertainty. He gave the impression that he knew that he had to see his doctor and he had to wait. Moreover, you could notice the normal tension that accompanies a doctor's visit. When he entered, he allowed the auscultation and opened his mouth without major difficulty. After the office visit we went to the pharmacy to pick up the medicine. Gabriel walked next to me observing everything. I felt delighted.

> - Cindy, today Gabriel behaved like a normal child at the doctor's office.

> - What are you talking about? What did he do?

> -He was very alert, looking at everything as if he wanted to make sense of what he was seeing.

Even I did not know how to explain it. That day I had a little of the Gabriel that I hoped I would be able to enjoy one day.

> -If you could have seen him, he was so alert!

We soon started to notice a gradual improvement. He would joyfully run out of school happily. I could go to the classroom to pick him up and I would always find him seated having his lunch. He would jump out of his seat. I would hug him and he would go for his backpack so we could leave. The teacher used to tell me that at a certain time he would already know that I would be arriving and he would become impatient.

He no longer looked tired and his joints started to strengthen. He started a process by which he sometimes had good days and sometimes bad ones, but the bad ones were lessening. They were almost always related to poor digestion or some of the foods he could not assimilate, such as eggs, grains and chocolate.

Since he was more conscious of his surroundings, one day we took him to the playground in downtown Wellington in Palm Beach, close to where I live. Gabriel was happy climbing giant doughnuts, sliding through strawberries, running on pancakes and spinning around in pineapple wheels! What a fantasy!

An obese lady with another lady, who had an oxygen tank, and two babies arrived. Since Gabriel passed close to them the obese lady got worried and said to us:

> - Your child is too big to be here. This is for little children.
>
> - What are you talking about? My son is 4, he is not bothering anyone; - my daughter answered.
>
> - It is not according to his age, but according to his height, -she said.

- The child is autistic, and you should be more considerate of others, - I told her.

She made a questioning gesture as if she did not know what I was saying. The other lady said something to her. She made an indifferent gesture and added:

-Then you should be attending to   him.

- Let's go, Mom, before I have a fight here, - said Cindy.

As we were leaving we passed the height measurer, Gabriel did not exceed the limit and the toddler's section was empty. Ignorant! This is what society counts on, I thought.

During one of the visits to the pediatrician, she referred us to a neurologist to assure ourselves that everything was good with his little head. They did all the tests again, except the MRI, because of the metal crowns he has in his mouth.

This time they did not have to put him to sleep, even though he was uncomfortable with all the cables they had placed on his head, he did not suffer as much as the first time.   All the exams were normal and the doctor referred us to a center for speech therapy, one of the best ones in the area.

At the school they had a graduation for them and I will, as long as I live, never forget the beautiful words that Gabriel's teacher spoke describing him;

> - "Gabriel is all love and sweetness for everyone. In our class we teach him the daily skills he needs to live…and he teaches us about life."

I know what she was talking about. Gabriel is a special being; he is an example of love and kindness, extremely sensitive to the pain of those who surround him. Gabriel is my angel.

Notes

CHAPTER 13

NOW WHAT?

Gabriel made a lot of progress at the school but he was already turning 5 years old and had to move to another school. The uncertainty and worries started all over again. Where will we take him? What organization or person would be trustworthy? They recommended a private school to us and we started the well known procedures.

By that time Gabriel was not doing his stigmatic auto stimulation any more, but he hadn't made any progress in speech. He spent the summer playing outside in his pool. He learned to ride a bike and recognized the dog's presence. We had not succeeded in taking away the DVD player from him. He was not interested in anything else.

When the new school year began, my daughter decided to limit his medications even more.

> -We have to force his body to work. He has been taking Nystatin for 2 and a half years and TMG for almost a year.

The first one she eliminated was Nystatin. After that went the enzyme and then zinc and finally IgG within two to three week intervals.

He started to have stomach ache and we started him on IgG again since that was the last one we eliminated. We continued with TMG, Culturelle, vitamin C and calcium. To avoid yeast we bought him a cream that contains caprylic acid, a derivative of coconut.

Before starting the chosen school, we visited it and noticed a lack of organization and materials. The person in charge said that they were in the process of remodeling. We saw only about 4 children and a teacher who was practicing effectively with one of them. We were impressed by the individualized instruction. They told us that there were 5 children with one teacher and two assistants. What most influenced our decision was that they assured us that Gabriel would learn from five to ten words by the end of the first month. To our understanding that was the only thing that was holding him back.

Gabriel was entitled to financial help, so the finances were not a determining factor. We decided to try.

The first week, as they had promised us, he said his first words:' tickles', 'banana' and 'ice cream'. We did not like the security and when he arrived there was no activity or pattern for him to follow. We decided to wait and see how it would unfold.

We noticed a small regression the second week. We thought it had to do with his adjustment to the new school, but when he had a bowel movement there were foam 'pellets' in his bowel movement. We immediately gave him baking soda and he continued eliminating them during the weekend.

I asked my husband:

- What is foam made of?

- From petroleum.

That weekend Gabriel lost his concentration and direction. On Monday I went to the principal or the person in charge of the center and informed her of what had happened. She went to the teacher:

- Take those pellets out of here, Gabriel took some!

Since he was a little under the weather with a cold, I took him to his pediatrician and told her about the incident.

> - That does not do anything. He eliminated them, right?

I do not know what I had expected. It is useless to try to make the doctors see that there is a possibility that these children are ingesting toxins that their bodies do not tolerate for whatever reason. Their surrounding environment is composed of constant harmful substances. It is everybody's duty to provide a healthy environment, but it is easier to shut your eyes or to assume an accepting attitude allowing yourself to be led by sheer inertia.

One afternoon my daughter went to pick Gabriel up from school and she arrived at the moment that he was coming out of the bathroom barefoot.

> - What are you doing in the bathroom without shoes sweetheart? Yuck, how gross!

Every time we left we worried more. We waited a while to see if things would improve, since we did not want to rush into a decision based on our past experiences.

Because Gabriel was not coordinating well, I stayed with my daughter during the weekend. On

Sunday afternoon I went home only to return on Monday. In the evening my daughter called me.

- Gabriel fell.

- Where? What happened?

- When he was going into the shower he slipped and fell backwards on the little cement wall where the shower door is.

- Did he hurt himself?

- Yes, he cried like never before. He hit himself in the middle of his back; he also hit his leg and cut his toe.

- What did you give him?

- I numbed the bruise with spray and put a cloth with Epson salt on him.

- Did he hit his head?

- No, he braced himself with his elbows.

- Good, watch him during the night to see if he has to be taken to the doctor.

The following day the bruise looked enormous. We decided to take him to the doctor, just in case. We signed him out so we could pick him up early.

When I arrived at the school the teacher was not in the classroom so I went to the cafeteria. I could not believe my eyes! Gabriel was standing on a chair with his back to the food, barefoot and jumping like a monkey. There were children all over the place, running, trying to get out, and teachers yelling at them, spaced out children…no, no, no.

The teacher stopped eating and approached me.

- I will take care of him, I said to her.

- I am going to get him a dry sweater.

I then noticed that he was all wet. His sneakers and socks were under the table. I changed his clothes and put on his shoes. I left there almost running. I felt like bursting out with laughter, I do not know if it was out of frustration or if it was because of what I had just witnessed.

- You're happy, huh? You are wild.

We arrived at the doctor's office and waited to be called. When we were walking in, I noticed that Gabriel had taken off his shoes and socks again. I put them on again.

- Don't take off your shoes. We do not do that, only at home.

The doctor looked him over and listened to his chest.

- The bruise is in an area with a lot of muscles. He walks well and responds to stimuli. His spine is fine.

When I arrived home I said to my daughter:

-Gabriel is beginning to speak, but I do not think his behavior is improving. There is neither structure nor discipline at school. If he remains there he will develop behavior problems. He acts normal, his behavior has improved a lot and we cannot risk that. His weakness is speech; we have to help him with that without impairing the other.

Cindy was pensive. She is very discreet. She is Gabriel's mother. In the end it was her decision.

She called my oldest daughter who is an elementary school teacher.

- Of course you can bring him here. It is an excellent program, I can keep an eye on him and if you need me to stay with him in the afternoon for whatever reason, I would do that. I can help you.

In the little town of Vieques, Puerto Rico, there is a saying that says: there were many of us and then the mule gave birth.

My daughter began to feel weak and had to go to the doctor. She was diagnosed with Lupus which affected her kidneys, which from my understanding is related to the tension she has. Now I understand my father's words as he was dying:

- "Cindy…"

-Yes, Dad, do not worry; I will take care of her.

- Not you, Our Lord.

- Of course, Dad, God.

When the day arrived for Gabriel's speech therapy appointment we were involved with my daughter's illness and we missed it. Now we will have to wait and see if we can get another opportunity. We are on the waiting list.

At this time Gabriel is attending the school where my daughter Aisha is working. Before leaving school, we had made arrangements for him to continue with his swimming lessons since that's what he liked best. He loves to swim and it is excellent therapy to improve his coordination.

When winter is over we will resume swimming classes. He used to get excited when I would go for him and we would head to the pool. He would run out of the car, run into the building where one registers, wait for me to sign and stand in front of the door waiting for it to open up. Then he would walked through the hallway, go outside, go around the pool to where his trainer was waiting. We look forward to this.

He is getting accustomed to the school and until now he has not given any indication that someone or something is bothering him. He is happy upon arrival as well as departure. He repeats sounds but does not articulate. Once in a while he says a word, but subsequently forgets it. He has verbally asked for help, follows directions and recognizes his teachers. Not all runs perfectly as we are human, but I do see that there is willingness to help, caring discipline, and a cooperation that far exceeds any momentary carelessness. His progress has been gradual, sometimes imperceptible to us who are with him day in day out. Nevertheless, people who saw him in the beginning do not believe that it is the same boy.

When I come to pick him up in the afternoon, he smiles at me. I never thought that a smile could be worth so much!

-Thank you, God, for that divine smile he has!

In September my son, Loren, moved to Florida with his family; Enrique, 11, Krystal, 9 and Keyli, four years of age. They lived in Cindy's house for two months with Gabriel.

Those were the most productive months socially, that Gabriel has had. They are three children with an admirably compassionate soul. They recognize Gabriel's condition and are willing to give up their wishes for him. They play on the trampoline holding hands, they wait for their turn, they wait for Gabriel, they direct him and teach him how to share and be aware of the people around him. How many adults could learn from Keyli's self denial.

During winter break Gabriel made a big improvement. He is more attentive, talkative and active in school. We are trying to determine what has provoked this new hope in order to be able to nurture it.

Notes

Notes

CHAPTER 14

THE FUTURE

Looking back, the scenes I remember make my soul tremble. I do not want to remember anything that I lived through. I just want to forget and enjoy our child, but a frightening thought haunts me every night. What happens with other autistic children? How are they treated? Who tries to help them? Who makes their life more bearable? What are they doing to prevent new cases from happening, how is the research coming along?

This syndrome is tearing away these children, out of their parents' arms. They are their most valuable treasures. To watch your healthy child become someone who does not even feel physical pain or whose mind is roaming in a void, constantly crying without knowing why, is an experience that tears away even the strongest spirit and leaves deep impressions on your being.

In the last two or three years, an educational campaign has been developed and many people understand that autistic children are special children who do not know how to act in this society, and who do not know how to do what is expected of them.

There are parents who run away from their marriage and flee from their responsibility. There are relatives who criticize or are angered because of jealousy or self-centeredness. Unfortunately, these children have no one. Sometimes even the doctors are not willing to try something innovative to seek another result.

Gabriel has improved a lot and I know that in time he will speak. His diet, supplements, detoxification and therapies have been determining factors. There is something only those who are close to him can give him, and that is a sense of security and trust. From all this caregivers emerge as people with more humility and compassion. With all of this we become closer to God and we recognize how helpless we are in the face of ignorance. In my desperation I wrote:

"God, I come before You,

with a heavy laden heart,

I have no more strength,

I am no more calm,

I need your loving care,

Under your holy arms,

I need your soothing love and

tender...

Would you comfort me, God?"

Today we are no longer the people we used to be. We have learned to appreciate that which we took for granted. We have established other priorities. We have developed patience, resignation, and wiped away our pain...

And Gabriel, not only has grown with us, but helped us to grow.

> - Thank you, God, for putting us in charge of this little angel. Thank you for having given him to us. Thank you for enabling us to help him. Thank you, because we know that Gabriel is happy!

Notes

CHAPTER 15

TO GABRIEL

Gabriel entered that tunnel at the age of 2 years and 4 months. He is walking towards the exit exactly three years and four months later. His joints are strong. His vision is alert. He smiles at us when we arrive. He asks for help through gestures. He invites us to accompany him, he takes the initiative to go out and play and so many more things that parents usually take for granted. I imagine that the exit is near.

> -One already sees the light, my little angel continue improving, continue struggling. You know what you have to do. You are going to overcome all these obstacles and emerge stronger.

At the end of the road there is a light of hope and triumph. May God bless you. Mom is here. Grandma is here. We are all here. We love you, Gabriel.

REFERENCE BOOKS

Lewis, Lisa. <u>Special diets for Special Kids.</u>
2 vols. Arlington: Future Horizons, 1998-2001

Shaw, William. <u>Biological Treatments forAutism
and PDD.</u> United States: 2nd ed. The Great Plains
Laboratories,2002

Schettler, Ted, et al., <u>In Harms Ways: Toxic Threats
to Child Development.</u> Cambridge: Greater Boston
Physicians for Social Responsibility, 2001.

Stock, Carol. <u>The Out of Sync Child.</u> New York:
The Berkley Publishing Group, 1998

ABOUT THE AUTHOR

The author of *My angel Gabriel* was born in Patillas, Puerto Rico. She has a Bachelor's degree in Arts from the University of Puerto Rico and completed her Master in Latin American Literature at Florida Atlantic University. She has dedicated most of her life teaching Spanish at a high school, although she has also taught in different fields. She retired prematurely from the Florida public school system to start a new career as a writer, but postponed her plans in order to dedicate all of her time, after the diagnosis, to the care of her autistic grandchild. The following three years include research about this condition.